You are perfect!

Return to your factory setting
Finn Underhaug

Contents:

About the author:

Finn Underhaug grew up in an industrial family, as the second youngest son of a factory owner in Jæren, Norway. He holds an MBA from Lund University in Sweden and has run his own investment company for several years. Finn has been actively engaged in a number of enterprises, such as advertising, printing, property investment, property development and membership companies. His primary focus as of today is health.

Preface:

The reason that I am writing this book is the discovery of something that has improved my life. I've gained access to a new understanding of how people operate on a mental level and how our lives are prevented from unfolding freely.

We are born with incredible resources, the source of wisdom, happiness, satisfaction and inner peace. Everyone can access these resources, but not many know how. They're not easy to discover unless someone points in the direction of how it all works. This understanding is a gift to all humanity, not a recipe for things you need to do or achieve. The intention of this book is to convey knowledge which can bring you new insight.

My deepest gratitude to everyone who has made this book possible, Arny, Dan Cato, my daughter Liv, my son Ådne, my wife Berit, Helen, Rasmus and Øyvind, who have read drafts and provided useful feedback. Thanks to Else M. Tungland who has contributed to the writing process, and Vibeke Høie-holgersen who provided color and illustrations to the text.

Finn Underhaug, Bryne, September 27th 2019.

Insight can change your life!

This is a book for everyone who feels like they're doing fine enough, but are lacking something in their lives. For those who are afflicted by stress, anxiety, depression, low self-esteem, insomnia and other problems, or who are simply curious about how humans operate on a mental level. The book is based on the discovery that there are three things that combined shape everyone's experiences – **Mind, Thought** and **Consciousness** – what we will refer to as **the three principles.** These are like a force of nature, something that affects us all equally, just like gravity.

The three principles were first described by Sydney Banks in 1973. He was a Scottish orphan who migrated to Canada, a working-class commoner riddled with low self-esteem and a faltering marriage. In an attempt to save their relationship, he attended a marriage seminar with his wife where they were encouraged to express their feelings and be honest with each other. Unfortunately they made little progress, and wished to leave. Banks explained to one of the therapists how torn he felt and how low his self-esteem was.

The therapist's answer was: "That's the most ridiculous thing I've ever heard in my life". Banks then realized that his self-esteem wasn't actually low, he just **thought** it was:

"All my insecurity is just a product of my own thoughts!"

He describes it as though a bomb went off in his head. An immense beauty entered his life when he realized how our thoughts and feelings arise, and how we experience life. He later explained this through the three principles.

Banks never claimed to have invented the three principles. He gained an insight which changed his life, an insight available to all, which can change your life too. I have experienced it firsthand.

This book is based on my own experiences and a wish to contribute with something that will help everyone discover which remarkable resources we are born with as human beings.

The yellow note

I can't complain about my life. I was brought up in a good home with a stable income, but from early on I sought answers to the meaning behind it all. Who are we, and what is our purpose? Since I was a child, I wondered why some people are quiet while others are outgoing. At school, some kids would be very loud while others were almost invisible. How do things turn out that way? I was curious about life's great mysteries, where we come from, and how things all relate to each other.

Later in life I sought answers in different places. I discovered a jungle of self-development books, a vast and disorienting jungle. There had to be some-thing simpler than this! I dipped into numerology, meditation, astrology, homeopathy and related subjects. In one of these events, I was given a yellow note by a friendly therapist. It changed my life. The note said "Sydney Banks". I went home, googled the name and started reading about the three principles. There was no textbook with steps to be taken or things to be done.

The principles guide us to insight in how our personal experience of life is created by thought. We all live according to our own ideas that are created when thoughts are formed in our consciousness. Our senses are like a Special Effects Department making our thoughts believable and real. Our thoughts and senses are connected. Everything we experience is our own thoughts. We all experience the world differently.

It was truly liberating to discover that there is no objective reality outside ourselves. All there is, is our thoughts about everything that's happening. There's no common perception of who Finn is. Everyone experiences their own version of reality.

This insight was the beginning of the big change.

"Mind, Consciousness and Thought. All is pure love."

— Sydney Banks

Listening to the words

The three principles can only be understood intellectually to a certain degree. You will gain more from this book if you're able to set aside your common assumptions of how things work, and try to open yourself to new insights. One word of advice is to listen to the words like you are listening to music.

Absorb the text and let it do wonders!

This is not a description of a method to be memorized. With new insights, you'll see how things change by themselves.

Even though the message is simple, it requires a new understanding of our reality on many levels, which can be hard to grasp.

There is hope for everyone.

You are not a victim.

You have the necessary resources for a good life.

All feelings are created by thoughts.

Thoughts are air – they're nothing.

You cannot be afraid of nothing.

*You feel only what you think
- your thoughts in the moment.*

You are not your thoughts. You are the thinker.

*You are not what is being thought.
You are what is observing.*

Through his universal principles, Sydney Banks gave us a gift. We try to explain the unexplainable, things you are given from birth and which are always a part of you, your perfect factory setting.

Have an open mind ...

What are the three principles?

The three principles are no method or tool describing which actions to take in order to have a better life. They are a guide to insight in how you function mentally, helping you rediscover the mental health you were born with. The three principles can be seen as something fundamental, like gravity. No one knows exactly what gravity is, but we have all experienced how it affects us directly.

The three principles are **Mind**, **Thought** and **Consciousness:**

Mind is the intelligence which brings everything to life – the child's mind, the factory setting we are all born with. It is the energy that fills you, the soul, some call it God. The energy we are all a part of. It is what makes flowers stretch towards the light and birds migrate to warmer places during winter. It show us what we are meant to be.

The Mind is an endless love which gives and gives without demanding anything in return. You only need to receive from it. The less you resist, the better it works.

Thoughts are created in the present. A continuous, endless stream of thoughts flow through us. This cannot be changed or stopped, but you can choose which thoughts to hold on to. Thoughts and thinking are two different things. Thinking is when you focus on a particular thought.

All experiences are created through thoughts in the present moment. Thoughts create feelings. We always feel what we think. Thoughts are not dangerous. Thoughts are not reality. All you experience is thoughts. When you start believing in thoughts, they will seem real to you, but in reality they are merely air.

Consciousness is the image on the canvas of experience, where thoughts are made real. The realization that I exist: senses, taste, smell, vision, hearing and touch, everything that allows us to experience anything. Together with thoughts, consciousness creates our reality. We sense what we think. Without thoughts, we have no senses.

It was wonderful to realize that I didn't need to do anything in order to change. When the three principles began to imprint themselves deeply in me, my life changed by itself.

"Your thoughts are like the artist's brush. They create a personal picture of the reality you live in."

— Sydney Banks

My thought-based reality

Each and every one of us lives in our own world of thoughts. That's why no one experiences things in the same way. We focus on different things. No one thinks the same way, therefore we experience situations differently.

We create our own world with our thoughts.
No one sees the world as you do.

Thoughts create feelings

If you react to something by getting angry, the feeling of anger is produced in your thoughts. The same goes for envy, fear of not being good enough, feelings of low self-worth, not being included, not being loved, and so on.

You might not be able to change your thoughts or stop them from coming, but you can choose which ones to hold on to. A thought only becomes real when you chose to believe in it. What we experience is our thoughts. When you let go of one thought, a new one will appear.

Thoughts aren't real in themselves, even though it feels that way when we believe in them. They're as real as a fantasy or a daydream. The more we believe in a thought, the more real it becomes and the feelings it creates.

Positive thoughts create good feelings.
Negative thoughts create bad feelings.

This doesn't mean that we aren't supposed to experience bad and difficult feelings in our lives, but there's no reason to get stuck in them.

"Thoughts are
not reality,
but it is through
thought we create
our own reality."

The illusion

We live in a world which has been created in such a magnificent way that we believe in it. My entire life, I believed I lived in a real world. I believed that my happiness and safety was a result of luck – having a good childhood, a stable income and of course, some of it was due to my own hard work. But I never doubted that the given circumstances dictated how I felt. Even when my happy circumstances seemed not to correlate to how I was feeling inside.

I tried explaining my state of mind with things I had experienced, which seemed logical. Lost love created bad feelings. Good financial results created a sense of joy and security – but there were exceptions.

Lost love didn't cause constant sadness. In the middle of the worst heartbreak, I could suddenly become occupied with something else which gave me good feelings. I thought time heals all wounds, this will pass too. But what did really happen? What happened was that I forgot to feel unhappy.

I actually stumbled into other thoughts. Later, I've understood how thoughts play a central role in how I feel. Yes, I do feel what I think, indeed. Thoughts are free, and we can choose which thoughts we want to keep.

Thoughts simply appear. We never know which one will appear next. Our mood changes according to our thoughts. That's how we work.

Thoughts are all-consuming. Everything we experience in life and call reality are really just our experiences of our thoughts about what is happening. Everything is a thought-experience, a psychological experience. That's why it's so important to understand how thoughts work.

"You can't even be aware of creation without the presence of thought."

— Sydney Banks

Thoughts are just "fluff"

The three principles are about letting go of all the ideas you have of yourself and the world around you. We all live in a thought-up world, our own illusion. Our senses, our consciousness and our thoughts are so magnificent that we experience them as real. But a thought, a fantasy and an illusion can't really do anything. They're just "fluff", as the Swedes say. Everything that is nothing can't do anything, even if it feels that way when you're in the middle of all the "fluff".

Everything changed when I discovered that my fluff wasn't serving anyone – not myself nor anyone else.

Seeing the truth is recognizing the illusion, the all-encompassing role that thoughts have in our lives. When you begin to understand the principles as an insight, you come back in touch with the mind, which is the source of truth. Then you can ride on life's rollercoaster knowing that there is a room inside you where all the power you were born with still lives.

Behind the thoughts there is love, wisdom, empathy, creativity and resilience, all of which we received the moment we were born, but only experience ever so rarely because we do not grasp that our thoughts are illusions.

The illusive thoughts are like clouds in the sky, passing by. It gets cloudy, but then the sun reappears. The sun is always behind the clouds.

Someone once said to me,
"Are you telling me that the chair isn't real,
that it's only thought?"

I said:
"Of course the chair is real.
But it comes to you via thought."

— Sydney Banks

You are not your thoughts

I am disappointed, I am sad, I am embarrassed, I am jealous, I am angry.

Unwanted feelings have many names.

The common assumption is that things outside us cause our bad feelings. As a result, we tend to blame others, and try to change the people we blame for our feelings:

Stop laughing, you're making me embarrassed!
Don't talk to me like that, you're making me angry!

Another reaction is blaming oneself, which can result in even more negative emotions:

I'm ashamed of having anxiety.
I'm sad for being angry.

When the feeling of anxiety leads to shame, the amount of negative emotions double. Then one enters a negative spiral. One can easily become trapped in dark thought patterns, growing darker the more attention we give them.

The three principles make us aware of such negative spirals by pointing to the fact that all feelings stem from thoughts. Feelings are thoughts. You aren't angry, you are holding a thought which provokes anger. It doesn't make sense to blame oneself or others for negative feelings. They're just thoughts. Thoughts are like air. They're not really worth our trouble!

Thoughts come from inside. No one can control the stream of thoughts. You have no reason to be ashamed of any of your thoughts. They aren't you. They are only your thoughts, which you can decide to hold on to or let go of. The more you hold on to thoughts which create negative emotions, the stronger those emotions get. It can be difficult to let go of these thoughts, but when you become aware of how things work, it will get easier. By gaining insight into the three principles, you will see the world from a new perspective and allow yourself to live with the entire spectrum of feelings, without being bothered by them.

Feelings are like a reset button, telling you that your thoughts are off track. Your natural state is satisfaction and joy.

jealous

unhappy

ashamed

angry

sad

scared

Breaking out of the thought-prison!

All feelings stem from thoughts. You think you're sad, and thereby feel even sadder. You think your self-esteem is low, which makes it even lower. We might even take this self-torment even further by identifying ourselves completely with our negative feelings when we make such claims as:

"I'm depressed and have low self-esteem."
"I'm an overly sensitive emotional wreck."

But you aren't your negative feelings.
Your feelings are just a product of your thoughts.

You are not your thoughts.
You are the thinker.
You are only experiencing your own thoughts.

The only thing stopping you from feeling good right now is your thoughts. You can't stop your thoughts. They keep coming in a steady stream, but you can choose which ones to hold on to and which ones to let go of. There is a difference between thoughts and thinking. The more you think about something, the truer and realer it feels.

Your true self is beyond all thoughts, a part of the eternal, unchangeable mind, this great, shapeless substance from which all living things spring. That is a nice place to be. Make your way back to your inner peace and clarity. Feel the mind lead you back on track. You don't need to make any changes in order to be happy.

You are perfect!

From outside-in to inside-out

Most of us live under the illusion that our experiences are created from the outside in. We believe that what happens around us decides how we feel, whether that be positive or negative. But according to the three principles, life is actually created from inside out.

This provides us with much more freedom, potential and power to meet life's challenges and live the life we really want. No matter your background, social status or circumstances, we're all born with the same, perfect factory setting.

My coworker is always angry and grumpy.
It's contagious, making me grumpy too.
For that reason, I'm unhappy at work.

Outside-in

Inside-out

My coworker is always angry and grumpy.
It must be because of his thoughts.
He is probably unhappy at work.

There's no use in blaming the weather any longer

Throughout my childhood I was defined by an exterior reality. It was all about being and doing what was expected of me. It was important to get a degree, a job, the right friends, the rights clothes and other material goods. When something went wrong, I had to take care of it. When I realized that my perception of the world wasn't real, I stopped caring so much about what other people expected. Then everything became more quiet. My stressful thoughts disappeared. I allowed myself to feel what I wanted, what really mattered. I stopped planning everything in detail, started listening more, living more, and got a better life.

I still have bad days where I find myself blaming my stress on exterior factors. I might blame my wife, the weather or a neighbor for stressing me out. It's not really the weather's fault, though, that I'm in a bad mood – it's my thoughts about what's happening. This might sound a bit simple, even naive. Should we really be unaffected by things outside ourselves? What if your boss calls you out for being irresponsible, lazy and self-absorbed after having sat up all night to meet a deadline? Surely that will effect your thoughts. You might have raging thoughts of the boss being an idiot, of never setting a foot in the office again, of posting a fitting description of said moron on Facebook.

Or you might get depressed: Even though I did as well as I could, it still wasn't good enough. I am incompetent, useless and having nothing to contribute to this world.

Or you can choose thoughts which make you calm, content and able to deal with your boss, who is obviously just having a bad day. I did my best, but maybe I still have something to learn? I am calm, prepared and aware.

Or you can think about whether this might be the right time to find a new job! When one door closes, another one opens. I am content, happy and excited about the next chapter in my life.

You cannot control everything that happens, but no matter what happens, your thoughts decide how you will feel. You cannot change the weather or your boss in order to feel better. Change begins with yourself and your thoughts, from inside.

"Achieving mental stability is a matter of finding healthy thoughts from moment to moment. Such thoughts can be light years or seconds away."

— Sydney Banks

From victim to owner

Sometimes you might catch yourself thinking that everything would be better if just the circumstances were better. That if you had more money, a nicer car and took vacations more often ... if only others had been more understanding, kind and generous. If only you were smarter, prettier and less insecure. The list could go on forever, but would we really be happier if the criteria were met?

You might have found that the vacation you were looking forward to didn't turn out as you'd hoped, or how quickly that rush of joy disappeared after finishing your last exam. Happiness is often short-lived. But still, you might keep thinking about everything that needs to change around you in order for you to feel good?

A good life isn't something one has to earn, or something one can buy for money. Being happy is a feeling you have inside when you feel confident and face challenges in an optimal manner. The good news is that this is your natural state of being. You always embody this power, and can always regain it simply by leaning back and listening. This is also the case in more dramatic circumstances.

At some point in our lives, we all experience the loss of a loved one, tragedies, accidents and pain. We cannot simply turn our heads away and pretend like it's not happening – but we can pause and find restitution in the power behind the thoughts. The only thing that is real is the moment.

We can also decide whether we want to submerge ourselves in negative thoughts, or if we want to treat all experiences as opportunities to learn from. Whether we want to be a victim of the circumstances or the owner of experiences which provide new insight, growth and change.

"Life is like any other contact sport; you're gonna get your knocks. But it's not the knocks that count, it's how you handle them. If you handle them with anger, distrust, jealousy, hate, this in return is what you're going to get. But if you handle these knocks with love and understanding, they don't mean much. They just dissipate."

— Sydney Banks

"Life is like any other contact sport; you're gonna get your knocks. But it's not the knocks that count, it's how you handle them."

— Sydney Banks

An accident seen from inside-out

Many people find that their lives changed after they learned about the three principles. I can't brag about having experienced dramatic epiphanies or huge crises. But we all have our challenges, no matter how big they are.

I was out driving one Sunday when, just as I was parking by a beach, my ears were cut by the sound of metal being squeezed together. Suddenly the car was wobbling on top of a big rock. It scratched and grinded the metal as I backed up. The result was a solid dent in the fender and the door. Tough luck.

Had this been a couple of years earlier, the rest of my day would have been ruined. In fact, I probably would have been in a bad mood for weeks. That Sunday morning, I suddenly found myself sitting in a damaged (yet still working) car – of course I was upset. But still, I knew that feelings are entirely made from the inside out, not the other way around. It wasn't the dented fender that caused me to be upset, but my thoughts about what had happened. The dent wouldn't disappear no matter how annoyed I got. The damage had already happened and was in the past. The future was nothing to fret about either. The solution was obvious – the car would have to go to a garage for repair, and it probably wouldn't be cheap. None of these things had to ruin this Sunday. I went for a walk on the beach, just as I planned, and enjoyed the lovely spring Sunday.

This doesn't mean we can think our way out of any problem. The dent was real, but all problems are relative. If we know how we work, our perspectives change, allowing us to deal with situations in a better way.

Each moment, we create our own experiences, from inside out.

Change that comes with insight

When I gained insight into the three principles and the way our psyche works, I started seeing myself and others in a new way. My understanding of things, my thoughts, all changed. My life changed.

If you start thinking new thoughts by reading this, your life will also change without you having to do anything. The change has already happened. Your life is shaped by thoughts. When the thoughts change, so does life.

A better version of myself

After I gained insight into the three principles, I've become calmer and more confident. I feel guided in the right direction.

I understand and trust that I am part of a larger whole, something we are all connected to, something which is always there. I no longer have as concrete goals and plans as before. I'm more attentive and aware.

I am more present.

My head is more silent & peaceful.

I acquire a better bond with other people.

I am more resourceful & decisive.

I am more direct when I meet other people.

I trust myself more because I know that everyone sees things differently.

I'm not afraid to speak out because I am calm and confident.

I have more patience.

I've become a better listener. Everyone has something to say as long as you give them space.

I am more observant and aware.

There's no need to stress out

You can be taught how to make a career for yourself, but not how to be happy. You can fix the facade, but not learn how to feel love. You can be involved with people, but intimacy, empathy and creativity come from inside. Still we are led to believe that if we're clever enough and tick all the right boxes, we'll be rewarded with wealth and happiness.

We are entertained by sports and reality TV where the winners are the quickest, best, prettiest and smartest. Many search for happiness in the wrong places. Generation after generation has been taught that happiness is something to be earned:

"Hard work pays off".
"Nothing in life is free".
"Keep your nose to the grindstone".
"The Devil makes work for idle hands".

The three principles teach us that our natural factory setting are enjoyment and being content. You don't need to prove yourself worthy of anything. You already have it in you. All you need to do is receive. When you commit to your natural factory setting, the things you need will come to you when you need them!

"There is an enormous difference between finding your own inner wisdom and adopting someone else's beliefs."

— Sydney Banks

From noise to clarity

There's always a steady stream of information flowing towards us through TV, radio, newspapers and social media. There are news, politics, accidents, protests, executive meetings in the UN, photos of a friend's dinner plate, a cousin's birthday and an approaching autumn hurricane. There are a lot of bad news, some good, and many mundane.

How important is all of this information really?

I became more aware of how much unnecessary stuff my head was filled with. Stuff I wasn't interested in, or could do anything about. It felt like others were deciding which things I was supposed to care about! All the impulses drained my capacity to think. They amounted to a lot of noise in my head, empty talk and focusing on the world around me. I started distancing myself from who I was and what I was meant to be, away from everything I really wanted to do.

When the noise disappears, silence and clarity arrives. When you stop thinking hard, you see things clearer. New thoughts emerge through clarity.
In clarity, you are the best version of yourself. Clarity is not emptiness.

Clarity is your factory setting, your child's mind. Through clarity, you have access to all of your best resources. Clarity is love, power, empaty, peace, freedom, happiness and creativity.

The opposite of clarity is delusion.

Clarity is presence.
Clarity is calmness.
Clarity is listening.

You are perfect!

Better without all "the labels"

As things became quieter, I stopped labelling everything and everyone – I stopped analyzing my own and other peoples' behavior.

Most people go to great lengths to build an acceptable facade. We adjust to expectations and do whatever it takes to fit into our own, little box. We sort people into ethnic and political groups, like good friends and bad friends. All of this stops us from meeting other people as fellow human beings. All we see is the label on the outside.

We all play many different roles, but behind each role is a unique person experiencing the world in their own way. Often we only see the label, not the potentially amazing person behind the facade.

How often have you cut short a possible friendship because you jumped to a conclusion about the other person?

How many good conversations have you missed out on because you thought you knew what the other person was thinking?

How much wisdom might have been missed because you never showed interest in "those kind of people"?

The three principles teach us that all people experience the world completely differently through their thoughts. At the same time, we are all built the same way and are part of the same essence. As soon as we realize this, and start listening to our own wisdom, we can sense the soul behind the facade.

If you meet the people on your journey with more curiosity, I can promise you life will become much more interesting.

The search for happiness

Being happy is often connected to external factors, usually things we don't have. Many people think they would be happier if they had more wits, more money, a better education, a better job, a smaller belly, a bigger house, and so on.

The problem is that a rich man isn't necessarily a happy man. A rich man can be afraid of losing his wealth if that's what he sees as his source of happiness. Of course life is easier without money problems, but if one doesn't have the ability to find peace in the moment, happiness won't come either way. It's easy to lose a sense of here and now and not to be present in one's own life.

"The happiness is within you,
not something out there."

Be present in life!

The only thing that exists is what is happening right now.

If you're very preoccupied with your past, it will distract you from reality in the moment. What has happened is nothing but a thought, created by your own consciousness. The same goes for the future.

If you keep worrying about the future, your attention will be directed at things that might never happen. Which means you've been worrying for no reason.

If you're always most worried about what to do tomorrow, you'll never be fully present in your own life. Instead you will be carrying out your life in a waiting room, and life itself will never really happen.

You might have heard about the two rich Americans who were on a tropical island, complaining about how lazy the natives were. They were looking at a local man lying in the shade of a palm tree, relaxing. When he heard them talking about him, he told them that he was resting because he had been up early fishing for his family dinner.

Sure, but you could have kept fishing?
Yes, but why should I?
Because you could sell the fish and buy a bigger boat.
Yes, but why should I?
Because then you could fish even more, buy and even bigger boat and export fish to the US!
Yes, but why should I?
Because you'd get rich!
Yes, but why should I?
Because then you could go on holidays, have great food and relax under a palm tree all day.
Yes, but that's exactly what I'm already doing.

The future and the past are only thoughts.
Be present in your life! Life is what's happening right now.

The restless one

(Jan-Magnus Bruheim: "Årringar" Oslo, Aschehoug 1987. Translated and rewritten by Else M. Tungland)

He has no time to stay
and no time to eye.
People he meets,
he never greets.
Many irons in the fire
to be fast is what he admires
Always a lot to be completed
The work increased when he succeeded
As the day draws near its end
He stands there, back bent
And asks: what did life give to me
and where did it all flee?
This is how he rushed through life
without seizing the light
A happiness followed his tracks
but couldn't reach the man who never relaxed.

Safety and happiness can't be bank deposited

A couple of years ago I lost a considerable part of my personal wealth. Money I had invested in stocks and funds disappeared over night. Several millions were gone when the market suddenly and unexpectedly plunged. Economically speaking, it was a small tragedy. To be fair, I had gone a long time with a feeling that I should do something, but I trusted others instead of my own gut instinct.

I felt the loss in my entire body and I was not comfortable with talking about it. It was humiliating. I felt like a failure. I was so shaken up that I couldn't sleep properly. I blamed both myself and others. This was before I knew about the three principles. Eventually I figured out that it was my own thoughts that were the problem. I didn't go bankrupt. I didn't really notice it that much in my daily life. Yes, I had lost the financial freedom, but still my problems were miniscule compared to what many other people experience.

In the bigger picture, I was still doing pretty well and didn't need to move or sell my car. I realized how pointless it was to stay up at night and tear myself apart over something I couldn't change. My worries were all about the past, which was out of my control now.

Maybe this incident was meant to teach me that worries are nothing but unnecessary thoughts. Happyness comes from inside myself, not from money in the bank.

"Man sacrifices his health in order to make money. Then he sacrifices money to recuperate his health. And then he is so anxious about the future that he does not enjoy the present; the result being that he does not live in the present or the future; he lives as if he is never going to die, and then dies having never really lived."

— Dalai Lama

Are you so worried about the future that you're unable to enjoy the present?

The power you are born with

"Mind is not brain. Neither is it a thing or a thought. It is a psychic force which acts as a catalyst and turns thought, whatever conscious or unconscious, into the reality you now see."

— Sydney Banks

The perfect creation

We humans are amazing creatures. The body with all its organs and functions, down to the cells, molecules and atoms, keeping us alive without us needing to do anything. If we get a scratch, it heals itself. We breathe without thinking about it, and our hearts keep beating.

I recently watched a documentary about the Antarctic featuring a colony of penguins. They all had small chicks. It was cold, -40 degrees Celsius, and a storm was whipping up. They lived far away from the coast, so their parents had to travel far to get food. While the adult penguins were gone, the chicks nestled together. Finally, the parents returned with food before they left their chicks for good. There they remained, all nestled up in a large group, far inland. Then something remarkable happened. The entire colony started moving. Still squeezing together, like one gigantic organism, they moved towards the sea. After days of wandering, they reached the coast. There they were, all of them, at the edge of the ice, until a frail little chick pushed his way through the crowd and dived into the ocean – his second natural element. Then the others followed. This is life, the life force which keeps all processes going, both in nature and in humans.

We are born into this world as perfect beings, equipped with exactly what we need to survive and thrive. But for some reason, we have a very different view when it comes to our psyche. We strive to be masters of our own minds, constantly struggling for perfection. But is this really necessary?

Mental health is all too often associated with diseases which need to be treated. We all have a built-in, perfect mental health, we just do not understand how it works.

The three principles teach us that we are born with a perfect psyche. Our true nature is to be loving, caring, peaceful, creative, resilient and joyful. Then we are raised and schooled with the best intentions. We learn that one has to earn money in order to enjoy, to perform in order to be valued, and make ourselves worthy of love in order to be included.

This can cause us to lose sight of the life force and our true selves. Our thought-constructed reality, with all its demands and expectations, block the source of true wisdom and happiness.

The answers lie in silence

Thousands of thoughts race through your head each day. The torrent of the mind is unstoppable. You always feel what you think in the moment. Your body, your feelings and your thoughts are interconnected. That's how we work.

After learning how the principles work, a lot of the thinking in your head calms down. Things become more silent. Calmness, balance, love and presence are our factory setting, something we are born with. Our mental health, our mental wellbeing, which we are meant to experience. The reason we can't see this is that we experience something else in the moment.

When the stressful thoughts decrease, calmness appears. When calm, you see things clearer. You might become aware of impulses from your intuition, which have been hidden behind other thoughts until now. You'll become aware of other people and possibilities. Maybe words will surface in your head, guiding you. After a while, you'll learn to distinguish between new, good thoughts from the calmness, and old thought patterns which you can let go of.

Feel the energy flow through you!

Allow the life force, your factory setting, the resources you were born with to come to the forefront. In that calmness, you will find your path.

"Relax. Stay still. Wait until the wisdom talk to you, as it will."

— Sydney Banks

The swinging pendulum between illusion and clarity

Things do happen! Occurrences are real, but we only perceive our thoughts. All we experience is thoughts.

We are closest to ourselves when we don't think too much – when we're simply present in the moment.

Imagine that the pram with your child accidentally rolls off the edge of the pier and falls in the ocean. Some people experience immense clarity in critical moments like this. You know what to do, and you do it. That's when you're 100% present in your own life.

When we aren't thinking about what has happened or what might happen, we see things clearly.

You might have experienced moments where everything felt perfect, where you wouldn't have changed a single thing. These moments come to us like small pearls of joy. They can come more often if you're ready to receive them. This is your natural state – the child's mind.

Life happens in the moment. Everything else is thoughts about the future and the past.

The pendulum swings between presence in the moment and the illusion of the future or the past. The more you're in the moment, the closer you are to yourself.

"I've had a lot of worries in my life, most of which never happened."

— Mark Twain

past

future

Now!

New thoughts on mental health

Mental health issues have become a public health problem. There are hundreds of diagnoses, most of which have in common that they lack an explanation.

What causes us to fall ill, and how do we get better again?

What if most problems are caused by the fact that we have misunderstood how things work?

"The difference between good and bad mental health is not in the nature of a person's thoughts, but the amount of time that person spends thinking them."

— Ingvard Wilhelmsen (2011)

Understand your own psyche

You might think that anxiety comes from various factors in your life – that stress is triggered by the things around you and that others are responsible for causing your worries. When you realize that all of this comes from inside, that it is created by thoughts, none of it will be as alarming anymore. The thoughts and feelings they create are nothing to be fought. Just accept what comes, and know that it will pass. All of it is just thoughts. There is nothing to be afraid of.

You don't need to clench your jaws and search for causes and explanations. Lean back and be present in your life. All discomfort might not disappear immediately, but the less you do about it, the better it gets. When your head becomes silent, things gradually disappear by themselves.

You might even have experienced being startled by your own shadow. You're out on a walk and feel like there's someone following you, and you become uneasy. When you turn around and realize that it's just your own shadow, your fear and stress decrease immediately. You don't have to analyze why you were afraid, or where the shadow came from.

A thought is like a shadow. Something that is always following you, which can be frightening, but which poses no real threat.

Stress and anxiety tells you that your thoughts have derailed from your factory setting. We can choose to stop spending time trying to understand why we feel the way we do. Feelings tell us how far away our thoughts have brought us. They're like a compass showing that we've gotten lost. It's a sign of your perfect mental health working exactly as it should.

Gaining insight into the way things work helps us understand our thoughts and the fact that they are what is bothering us. The more relaxed you become when confronted by hard feelings, the quicker they go away. You aren't meant to change your thoughts, but simply understand how they work, then the change will come by itself.

"Going back into the negative past to find happiness is like trying to make a silk purse out of a sow's ear."

— Sydney Banks

Thought pits

We think about the past, about what could be different, what we should have said and done.

We worry about what others think of us, about things that annoy and hurt us. The more we think about it, the stronger it gets. It becomes realer, truer, worse and worse. That way we dig ourselves into our own thought pits, which deepen the longer we dig.

Thoughts about the future can also become thought pits. We think about everything that might happen, everything that needs to be done. How often don't we worry about things that never end up happening? We have busy lives, and the more we think, the less we get done.

Many people fall ill because of their own worries. Their thoughts become more than they can handle. Sometimes they treat the uncomfortable thoughts with medicine.

What if they had known that there's no use thinking about the past. No matter what you have experienced, it now only exists in your own thoughts. You don't need to linger by any of the heavy thoughts that come your way. Let them go, and let new thoughts arrive. Feel how things are fine right now. The moment is the only thing that matters, what you fill it with becomes your reality.

Does that mean we should stop planning and looking forward to things? No, but we should become aware that thoughts about the future create expectations. And behind each disappointment, there's an unfulfilled expectation. It might feel like other people create our expectations, but it all happens in our own thoughts. We need to be open to the fact reality won't necessarily unfold the way we had planned. That's the way it's meant to be, and it's okay like that.

Be open to surprises. They are what make life exciting. Then you'll be present in life, from moment to moment.

Trauma

People who have been involved in or witnessed episodes which can be experienced as life-threatening, may suffer from the effects later. Violence, bullying, war, traffic accidents or the sudden loss of a loved one can cause flashbacks, nightmares, sleep deprivation and loss of concentration. Trauma is often treated through psychotherapy and medicines. Many people drop out of treatment because they find it difficult to talk about what happened to them.

Some are diagnosed with Post Traumatic Stress Disorder (PTSD). They might constantly be feeling jumpy, becoming easily irritated or angered. These reactions may also manifest themselves physically in tense muscles, headaches and digestive problems. This is your body doing what your mind is telling it. Your perfect mental health is working the way it's meant to.

Denying bad experiences does not help us. Whenever we are chased by a tiger, we get scared – we're meant to get scared – but when the tiger disappears, the danger does too, and so should our fear. The only thing remaining is the thought of the tiger. Thoughts are constantly with us, and the feelings they create must be acknowledged, not denied. When we recognize that our feelings are being created by thoughts, they become less frightening. It's not always easy to see where bad feelings come from, but know that they are always created by thoughts.

Trying to analyze trauma leads us to re-experiencing trauma. We animate our experiences through our thoughts. Though there's no external danger, you are afraid because you are tricked by your own thinking. You misinterpret the thought and take it for real. But the trauma is in the past, not in the present. All that exists here and now is your thoughts. The feelings that arise when you think about it, are triggered by the thoughts, not by anything terrible actually unfolding in the present moment. Thoughts are just an illusion, nothing to be afraid of. See your thoughts, let them go, and gradually they will disappear.

"If the only thing people learned was not to be afraid of their experience, that alone would change the world."

— Sydney Banks

Recognize your thoughts,
and gradually the
feelings will let go.

Depression can be a sign of good health

Our thoughts create our problems, and our thoughts solve our problems. All problems are created by thoughts.

If you have destructive thoughts, it makes no sense to go over them again and again. If you are depressed and worn-out, it might be a sign that your thoughts have taken a wrong turn. When your muscles stiffen, your sleep diminishes and the stress causes your body to tremble, your thoughts have definitely veered off. These signs are a healthy reaction, our body trying to show us what's wrong. When we understand that, we automatically return to our factory setting.

Each day, thousands of thoughts fly through our heads. Some are positive and some negative. You can decide which thoughts you want to keep. This is why we have free will. A beautiful memory brings you good health, while a bad memory can cause trouble. You don't need to give your bad thoughts any further attention. Most of the things we worry about cannot be changed anyway.

Sydney Banks advises us to forget thoughts which cause difficulties and try to forgive ourselves and other people. When a person suffers because of a tough past, it doesn't help them to keep returning to the past in their thoughts. Doing so only causes more pain. What the person truly needs is love and compassion, for them to heal from the trauma. If you teach them that their sufferings only survive through their continued thoughts of suffering, they can start healing immediately.

"If you're in trouble with your thoughts there's no sense in digesting them over and over again. You forget them, you forgive yourself. You have to learn to forgive yourself and other people, and unless you forgive, you'll go through life in a hell hole, to put it bluntly. And if you look with logic, you'll see what I'm talking about is common sense."

— Sydney Banks

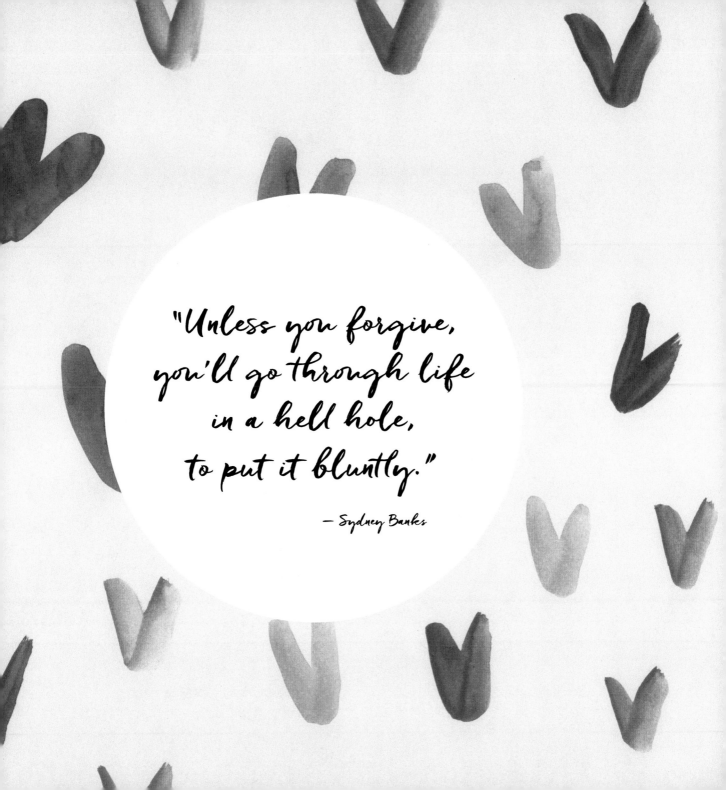

"Unless you forgive,
you'll go through life
in a hell hole,
to put it bluntly."

— Sydney Banks

A paradigm shift

A paradigm is a framework of basic assumptions within certain scientific disciplines, for example our understanding of the earth not beeing flat and gravity being what causes apples to fall from trees. A new paradigm involves a radical change of how we think about things.

The three principles offer a new paradigm of how we understand our mental health, our thoughts and our personal presence in the world.

Peace in our hearts, Peace on the earth

You don't need to change the world outside yourself in order to feel well. The world is created in your thoughts. If everyone understood the three principles we would never have any reason to argue about anything.

The three principles offer us insight as to how we can find our way back to our factory setting, which are well-being, peace and love.

Society consists of individuals. When people feel well, they spread peace and harmony. The outer world reflects the inner life of individuals. Peace in people's inner selves can create peace on the earth.

"If we can forgive everyone, regardless of what he or she may have done, we nourish the soul and allow our whole being to feel good. To hold a grudge against anyone is like carrying the devil on your shoulders. It is our willingness to forgive and forget that casts away such a burden and brings light into our hearts, freeing us from many ill feelings against our fellow human beings. "

— Sydney Banks

"It is our willingness to forgive and forget that casts away such a burden and brings light into our hearts"

— Sydney Banks

Use your energy in the right places

Much of what happens is outside of your control. You can't think your way out of famine and disease. If you stay under water too long, you drown. If dad is violent, mom is crying and the children aren't being fed, we have a real problem requiring action. But not everything can be changed. How you feel inside always depends on your thoughts and attitudes towards what is happening.

If you become seriously ill, it won't help you to think about how unfair it is that you got ill. You won't recover by being bitter, anxious and reclusive in addition to being ill.

It won't help children on the other side of the planet that you lie awake at night and think about them. On the other hand, if you're healthy, awake and in good shape, you can start fundraising.

Planes will crash regardless of whether the passengers inside are being ridden with phobia or enjoying the view with free drinks.

The less you fret about things out of your control, the more present you are in your life, and the clearer you will see how to handle the present.

"God,
grant me the serenity
to accept the things
I cannot change,
the courage to change
the things I can,
and the wisdom to know
the difference."

— Reinhold Niebuhr

A quiet revolution

Instead of the idea that everything that affects us comes from the outside, we learn that everything we experience comes from the inside. The only thing we experience is thoughts. Thoughts are just thoughts, they aren't dangerous. You are not your thoughts. You are the one thinking.

The simple understanding can revolutionize the kind of therapy which has insisted that you need to understand the cause of trauma and other problems.

According to the three principles, it is worthless to dig through the past in search of solutions. You don't need to understand the roots of your thoughts. They just appear, and you cannot control that. The most important thing to understand is how the thoughts behave, and the fact that you can choose which ones to keep and which ones to let pass.

The point isn't that you should always be on cloud nine. Life isn't always easy. Sometimes you might choose to linger by thoughts which cause grief, longing, fear, anxiety and feelings of inferiority.

The entire spectrum of feelings is a part of human life. They are what makes us feel alive. That's why it is perfectly natural to accept painful thoughts every now and them. Welcome them, notice how they affect you, then let them pass. If you meet hard thoughts with accept, and don't try to flee from them or avoid them, they might visit you less often. Their power will fade over time. Thoughts which cause pain aren't dangerous. They're just thoughts!

What would the world look like if everyone realized that they didn't have to avoid thoughts which cause negative feelings, and that they didn't have to change others in order to feel good themselves?

Do you want to change the world?
Start with yourself, and experience
a silent revolution coming from inside.

Mind your own business, or as we say in Norway:
sweep outside your own door, before you blame
others.

Plant a seed

Plant a seed, water it, tend to it. Then it will sprout and grow. After a while it will turn into a large tree which over time can become a great forest.

You are like a seed. You can grow to become great things if you allow your real self to sprout.

Abandon your old ideas of who you think you are and what you are raised to be. Leave the shell that is enclosing you, keeping you in place.

You are so much more than the notion of what you can be, should be, must be and everything you try to be. You're part of a powerful, unchangeable power, the source of all life, a limitless energy of resources which are always there, ready to fill you. You will feel it when you escape the fog of thoughts. It is always there, it's there right now.

The seed will sprout all by itself if only you let the sunlight in!

You are perfect!

Freedom to choose

The three principles tell us something about how things are made. Everything comes from the shapless. All we experience is what takes shape in our thoughts.

Our senses exist, but they reach us through our thoughts. You can only feel pain when you think. Without thoughts, no experience.

Facades and external noise, everything we thought was true, are only thoughts, only illusions.

Mental structures don't mean anything. They reduce our ability to be free and make independent choices which serve ourselves and others the best.

Creation is shape, transience. What created life was the shapeless, the divine, pure love, the true and eternal.

An example of how perspectives and lives change in light of the three principles.

OUTSIDE IN	INSIDE OUT	CONSEQUENCE
An objective reality.	Unique realities.	
An objective reality exists.	Everyone lives in their own thoughts.	Acknowledging that we see the world differently.
There are many idiots who don't understand what's going on.	Thoughts work in the same way for everyone, but everyone thinks differently and experiences reality differently.	Being patient with those who hold different views than ourselves.
I need to convince others that I'm right.	By understanding how my own thoughts work I can understand and respect how others experience things differently.	Learning more from meeting people with greater openness.
I need to do what it takes to fit in.	I am unique and I know inside my quiet inner self what is right for me.	I have the courage to publish this book.
Goals and performance	Clarity and peace	Insight
Results are reached through goals and hard work. I strive to reach my goals and everything that is expected from me.	I need peace and clarity to find my path. When my head is peaceful, the answers appear.	I am not passive and devoid of personal goals and ambitions, but aware of which things influence me when I have a calm mind.

OUTSIDE IN	INSIDE OUT	CONSEQUENCE
Victim.	A unique flower.	Bloom
I am a victim of external circumstances.	Our reality is created and recreated moment by moment through thoughts.	Choose freely between thoughts.
I am traumatized.	Bad memories exist only in your thoughts.	Circumstances may not change, but your experience of them will only change when you change what you choose to think about.
I am controlled by demands, stress and outer pressure.	I am guided by my own thoughts from inside.	I can do what I really want and what feels right for me.
Hustle and bustle	Inner peace	Insight
I am content when I perform.	I can find serenity. And be content without the hustle	Hustle and bustle will make the good feeling invisible.
I am angry.	I have thoughts of matters that make me angry. I am not my thoughts. Thoughts are not dangerous.	I can let go of that feeling. I do not need to act on my thoughts.
I am envious.	I have thoughts which make me feel envy. I am not my thoughts, I have nothing to be ashamed of.	I can let my thoughts pass. Thoughts are air. They are nothing.

Sources:

Banks, Sydney (2001) "Oneness of Life", foredrag Oahu, DVD.
Banks, Sydney (1998). "The missing link: Reflections on philosophy and spirit" Lone Pine Publishing , Canada.
Banks, Sydney (2001). "The enlightened gardener". Vancouver, BC, Lone Pine Publishing, Canada.
Banks, Sydney (2012). "Truth Lies Within", Part 2 of the Long Beach Lecture Series, Lone Pine Publishing, Canada.
Banks, Sydney (1987) "Second Chance". Lone Pine Publishing, Canada.
Bruheim, Jan-Magnus (1987). "Årringar" Oslo, Aschehoug.
Shapiro, Fred R. (April 28, 2014). "Who Wrote the Serenity Prayer?" The Chronicle Review.
Wilhelmsen, Ingvard (2011). "Det er ikke mer synd på deg enn andre". Hertervig forlag .

Web:

http://sydbanks.com
https://sydneybanksproducts.com/sydney-banks-quotes/
https://www.azquotes.com/quote/849375
https://www.overallmotivation.com/quotes/dalai-lama-quotes-compassion-health-peace/
https://www.devilinagoodman.com/post/2019/03/06/130-sydney-banks-quotes
https://www.goodreads.com/quotes/201777-i-ve-had-a-lot-of-worries-in-my-life-most
https://www.vg.no/nyheter/meninger/i/VRbqpJ/den-farlige-offerrollen
http://www.procrastinationpublications.com/295705287
https://thethreeprinciples.blogspot.com

Copyright © Troll As
Author: Finn Underhaug
Consultant: Else M. Tungland
Graphic design and illustrations: Vibeke Høie-holgersen
www.duerperfekt.no
1. edition